Your Situational Sanctuary:

Encountering God Beyond Church Walls

LISA SIMS

Copyright © 2014 Lisa Sims

The Business Professional Network

PO Box 1106

Conyers, GA 30012

ISBN-10: 0983232822
ISBN-13: 978-0-9832328-2-7

DEDICATION

This book is dedicated to my son, Timothy D. Sims, Jr., who God blessed me with when doctors said it was not possible. God made an impossible situation possible to reveal his power and glory. He used you to not only increase my faith but also show that despite how bad a situation may look, there is nothing too hard for God as long as you trust and believe. You are a living miracle as well as an example of what mustard seed faith can produce. I love you!

CONTENTS

ACKNOWLEDGMENTS

I would like to thank God for giving me the idea for the book while pouring into me the words for the book. Without Him, this book would not be possible.

Special thanks and love to my family for supporting me on my author journey.

I also would like to thank Vikki (Vikncharlie) at Fiverr.com for creating an awesome book cover design.

INTRODUCTION

When praise and worship saturate the sanctuary, isn't it easy to feel and identify God's presence? It feels like God entered the building and took a seat. The order of service no longer matters because the Holy Spirit is now the presider. You find the sermon ministering to your soul as if you and God are enjoying an intimate conversation over lunch. The minister extends the invitation to discipleship followed by a benediction. The service ends and fellowship begins. What happens when everyone goes home, and your temporary relief from your situation is over and you must return home to face it? What do you do? Can you still experience God's presence outside of the sanctuary as you did inside?

Some of my most memorable encounters with God occurred during the darkest times of my life. During those times, I could not see how "all things work together for good to those who love God, to those who are the called according to *His* purpose" (Romans 8:28). It was only after maturing spiritually that I learned the true meaning of that Scripture and how it was applicable to my situations. When it seemed as though He was absent, God appeared during my periods of unemployment, financial distress, sickness, death and childbirth. During these "situational sanctuaries," I learned not only about myself but also about God's awesome power.

Believers regard the sanctuary as a place of reverence. Dictionary.com defines it as "sacred or holy place" or "an especially holy place in a temple or church." I think of it as a place of refuge from life's storms. No matter how bad the winds of life's storms blow upon you, you can find shelter in the sanctuary. When all hell is breaking loose, it can be difficult to view your situation as a sanctuary but God is always present and waiting to help. Even in the Judean wilderness, David expressed his love for God and recognized the sanctuary's importance:

> *O God, You are my God;*
> *Early will I seek You;*
> *My soul thirsts for You;*
> *My flesh longs for You*
> *In a dry and thirsty land*
> *Where there is no water.*
> *So I have looked for You in the sanctuary,*
> *To see Your power and Your glory.*

Psalm 63:1-2

In *Your Situational Sanctuary*, you will learn how to transform life's situations into intimate encounters with God. Everyone experiences situations but not every situation results in an encounter with God. Although the opportunity presents itself, many never encounter God, experience His power or grow closer to Him. Don't let this be your story. You will also learn that whatever situation you face, place it in God's hands. Oftentimes, we focus too much on the situation rather than our Savior, Jesus Christ. 1 Peter 5:7 says "casting all your care upon Him, for He cares for you." Why not trust God with your situation?

Are you ready to embrace your situational sanctuary today?

1. IDENTIFYING GOD IN YOUR SITUATION

In the midst of your situation, sometimes it can be difficult to feel God's presence. Depending on your situation's severity, it is not uncommon to feel alone, hopeless and powerless and wonder whether God sees or even cares. The disciples experienced this in Mark 4:35-41 when they encountered a storm on the sea while Jesus slept. Although Jesus was with them on the boat, they did not recognize who He was or His power. Their response in Mark 4:41 confirms this:

And they feared exceedingly, and said to one another, "Who can this be, that even the wind and the sea obey Him!

In 2001, I found myself in a similar storm as the disciples except I was the only person in the boat. While working as a Web Developer Consultant at a telecommunications company, I heard rumors that no consultant wants to hear: budgets cuts. When budget cuts occur, consultants are among the first released. One morning, my manager called me in his office and delivered the devastating news that I was being let go. Talk about feeling sick to my stomach. It could not have come at a worse time because I was planning my wedding along with other financial responsibilities. What was I going to do? How could this be happening? When I arrived home from work, I felt so low that I skipped dinner and went to bed. Where was God?

We know God is omnipresent, omniscient, and omnipotent, but it does not stop Satan's scheme of trying to make us forget it. Satan is crafty. He plants a variety of thought seeds in our minds to convince us to doubt God and His love for us. In the same way that flowers need fertile soil, fertilizer, and water to grow, Satan knows that his seeds need the same. It is at these times that we must know and stand on God's word. Satan is a liar (John 8:44) and the author of confusion (1 Corinthians 14:33). If not careful, these thought seeds will take root, grow, and blossom and you begin slowly to doubt God and his promises.

Every person receives a measure of faith (Romans 12:3). Regardless of how much faith you have, it will be tested. Remember the saying "Faith that cannot be tested cannot be trusted?" This situation was my test. At 27 years old, I had experienced some storms but nothing of this magnitude. Satan began planting seeds of fear and doubt in my mind. Similar to the disciples, I did not recognize Jesus in my situation. I prayed to God for help with my situation, but I also had a backup plan. It was only years later that I realized that when you fully believe and trust God, you do not need a backup plan.

With my last day rapidly approaching, my consulting company contacted me about a possible new assignment. As I listened to the details of the new assignment, I was hesitant about its location but needed a job. Was this God answering my prayer? Was this the door opening while the other one was closing? My consulting company wanted to gain this company as a new client to place more consultants there and increase their profits. They desperately needed me to interview for the position and get hired. I reluctantly agreed. The interview went well, and the client selected me but I was not interested in the position. The commute was 50 miles one way requiring me to spend a considerable amount of time in Atlanta's rush hour traffic. I needed a job, but this may not be the one. What do I do?

While I prayed and read my bible for guidance, my consulting company aggressively pressured me to accept the assignment. They wanted this new client no matter the cost and did not care what it took to get them. They even stooped so low as to use my upcoming wedding to manipulate me to accept the position. They assumed that I would not have enough money to get married without a job. I felt like a pawn on a chessboard being used to capture the queen: the new client.

Where was God? I was at a crossroad and desperately needed guidance. I knew God was present, but I did not know or understand how to identify Him. Which way do I go? What decision should I make? When my consulting company saw I was not going to accept the assignment, they used their last pressure tactic: money. They offered me a bonus in addition to my salary to accept the assignment for one month. We negotiated a substantial bonus along with three months of salary after the assignment ended. I could not believe it. Even though I did not understand how to identify God in my situation, I knew no one but God could have orchestrated such a deal. I accepted the assignment for one month, received my bonus and three months salary, and was laid off but received unemployment until I found another job.

What is my point? God gives everyone free will to

make decisions. He guides but you must be willing to seek Him, listen for His voice, and follow His direction. In my situation, I hurriedly made my decision based on the available information. Knowing what I know now, I should have taken the time to get in a quiet place and meditate on the situation and listen for God's voice and direction. My hesitation and uneasiness were God's way of telling me not to accept the position, but I ignored the signs. If it were the right position, peace would have replaced my uneasiness.

My situation became a sanctuary because I needed an answer from God. I had a spirit of expectancy. I already had a relationship with God, but it is something about trouble that will send you running into God's arms. Although Psalm 46:1 says, "God is our refuge and strength, a very present help in trouble," you need to make sure that you have established a relationship with God before trouble comes. God is the best resource to have in any situation, but you still have a responsibility in the situation. Sometimes you may feel if you pray and "cast all your care upon Him, for He cares for you (1 Peter 5:7)," you are finished. Although God is omnipotent, you still must do those things that He expects you to do. He can open doors that no man can shut, but you have to take the first step in faith and put your hand on the doorknob.

Believers must realize that God can appear in unexpected ways and forms. Balaam did not expect God to use his donkey to talk to him (Numbers 22:28) and neither did Naaman expect God to use his maid for his leprosy healing (2 Kings 5:1-4). Be mindful of the various ways God can speak to you but remember this: Use the power of discernment to identify whether the message and messenger are truly from God.

2. PRAYING IN YOUR SITUATION

Isn't it easy to pray and rejoice when everything is going well? It seems that you have the Midas touch and everything your hands touch turns to gold. What happens when a tornado pops up in your life and threatens to destroy you and everything in its path? Whether the tornado is an illness, job loss, foreclosure, divorce or death of a loved one, you are in the direct path of the storm. Can you still pray and rejoice?

No matter how often or much you tithe, read your bible or attend church services, you will experience storms. Once you accepted Jesus Christ as your Lord and Savior, Satan put you in his crosshair and made you his target. 1 Peter 5:8 tells us "Be sober, be vigilant; because your adversary the devil walks about like a roaring lion, seeking whom he may devour." John 10:10 also states "The thief does not come except to steal, and to kill, and to destroy." If you are not careful, you may find yourself asking God "Why did this happen to me?" Matthew 5:45 reminds believers "for He makes his sun rise on the evil and on the good, and sends rain on the just and on the unjust." No one is exempt, but God gave us hope through Jesus as stated in the latter part of John 10:10: I have come that they may have life, and that they may have it more abundantly.

Trouble will knock on your door, walk in, and take a seat. Not what you wanted to hear, but it is the truth. John 16:33 says:

In the world you will have tribulation; but be of good cheer, I have overcome the world.

In life, trouble occurs for one of three reasons: you caused it (self-inflicted); someone else caused it (guilt by association), or no reason at all. Remember our friend, Job? Job was "blameless and upright, and one who feared God and shunned evil" (Job 1:1). He did nothing to cause his trouble, but he still became a victim.

During times of trouble, it can be difficult to pray. Depending on the severity of the situation, it may require all of your strength to cope with it. 1 Thessalonians 5:17 encourages us to "pray without ceasing" but sometimes trouble shocks you so bad that you want to pray but cannot find the words. You feel dazed and uncertain of what to do. At these times, prayer becomes critical. It is the best weapon that believers possess. Without prayer, you have no power because you are fighting with your limited strength instead of with the infinite strength of the Holy Spirit.

Prayer is your personal conversation with God. Oftentimes, we feel like we have to pray a certain way to get our prayers through to God. There are certain prayer guidelines, but this is not always the case. Prayers do not have to be eloquent to be effective but must possess two key ingredients: sincerity and right motives. Jesus warned his disciples about this in Matthew 6:5-13:

And when you pray, you shall not be like the hypocrites. For they love to pray standing in the synagogues and on the corners of the streets, that they may be seen by men. Assuredly, I say to you, they have their reward. But you, when you pray, go into your room, and when you have shut your door, pray to your Father who is in the secret place; and your Father who sees in secret will reward you openly. And when you pray, do not use vain repetitions as the heathen do. For they think that they will be heard for their many words. Therefore do not be like them. For your Father knows the things you have need of before you ask Him.

Jesus goes on to instruct them in the way they should pray known today as The Lord's Prayer.

God knows, sees, and understands everything. When Peter was sinking, he prayed one of the shortest prayers in the bible "Lord save me" and Jesus responded.

I recall a time in my life when it was difficult to pray. In October 2007, my husband, Timothy, and I learned that we were expecting our first child. We were so excited and could not wait to become parents. I traded my consultant job to start a new full-time Webmaster job for a state agency to be closer to home and my doctors' visits. Everything seemed to be going well.

In January 2008, I had a routine doctor's appointment and would find out our baby's gender. I was 20 weeks pregnant. Instead of finding out our baby's gender, we received devastating news. The high-risk specialist told us that our baby was not going to survive, and we needed to terminate the pregnancy. His words were void of emotion and cold as ice. It was as if he had seen this so many times that he was immune to it and ready to see the next patient. I felt numb and cried hysterically. How could this happening? What went wrong? Where was God? How could God allow this to happen?

As Timothy walked me out of the office to my car, I could not believe what had just happened. What was supposed to be one of the happiest moments of my life turned into a nightmare. We drove separately to the office, and I had to drive myself home. On the drive home, tears streamed down my face while I tried to keep my car in my lane. Once I arrived home, I walked upstairs to our baby's room, sat down on the storage box, and placed my head in my hands in disbelief. I tried so very hard to pray, but it felt like I had the biggest lump in my throat. I had no words.

Over the next several days, I tried to get a second opinion while my OB-GYN called me to discuss next steps. I returned to work and did not discuss my situation with anyone. While at work, my brother sent me a text message with a passage of Scripture to comfort me but instead brought tears to my eyes. I immediately proceeded to the bathroom because I did not want anyone to see me crying. As I closed the stall door behind me, I began to cry uncontrollably. The bathroom stall became my sanctuary. I began praying and thanking God for the gift He had given me but confessed that I didn't understand why this was happening. I did not want my baby to suffer. At that moment, I told God that whatever decision he made I would have to learn to live with it even though I did not understand it. A few days later, I went to my OB-GYN appointment and found out our baby's heart had stopped.

James 5:14 asks:

Is anyone among you sick? Let him call for the elders of the church, and let them pray over him, anointing him with oil in the name of the Lord.

At the time, I belonged to one church but visited another, which made it difficult for me to call on the elders. There will be times when you will have to pray for yourself and others because the elders are unavailable, or you cannot reach them in time. To withstand life's storms, you need a consistent and strong prayer life paired with daily bible reading. If you do not know the promises of God, you cannot pray in the Spirit, remind God of his promises, and rebuke the devil.

God gave believers power through his son Jesus. In Matthew 10:1, Jesus gave his disciples "power over unclean spirits, to cast them out, and to heal all kinds of sickness and all kinds of disease." You are a disciple of Christ. He equipped you for the battle, but you must stay connected to your commander: Jesus. In a physical war, soldiers communicate with their commander regularly to give updates and receive further instructions. The same applies to believers. To receive further instructions and strategies from God, you must communicate with Him on a daily consistent basis. Remember the saying: Little prayer, little power; much prayer, much power? John 15 describes the relationship of believers to Christ but meditate on these key verses:

If you abide in Me, and My words abide in you, you will ask what you desire, and it shall be done for you. By this My Father is glorified, that you bear much fruit; so you will be My disciples. As the Father loved Me, I also have loved you; abide in My love. If you keep My commandments, you will abide in My love, just as I have kept My Father's commandments and abide in His love.

John 15:7-10

Having a strong relationship with God along with a strong prayer life ignites your spiritual power. You also need a strong prayer circle that can intercede on your behalf when you cannot pray for yourself. Many of life's situational sanctuaries are not elaborately decorated, pleasant smelling or clean environments. Ushers, deacons, or preachers will not be available to greet and assist you. There will only be two people there: you and God. In my situation, a bathroom stall became my sanctuary. I invited God into my sanctuary through prayer, and He met me at my place of need. He also sent the Holy Spirit to comfort me during my discomfort. He will do the same for you and your situation. James 4:8 encourages us to "draw near to God and He will draw near to you." When was the last time that you drew near to God?

God answers every prayer. When I was a children's Sunday School teacher, one of my students told me that his father told him that God answers every prayer. I agreed and told him that I discovered that God may not answer our prayers the way we expect or when we expect. Mary and Martha are a good example. They sent for Jesus when Lazarus was sick, but Jesus did not arrive until Lazarus had died and been in the grave for four days and started decomposing (John 11). Jesus loved Lazarus so what took him so long? Jesus already knew that Lazarus was sick along with the outcome. Your situation may stink like Lazarus, and your response may be the same as Mary and Martha but remember God can still move in the worst of situations.

At times, you may feel as if your prayers are landing on deaf ears but God hears, sees, and cares. When praying to God, you not only need the right spirit (Psalm 51:10) but also need to be specific. James 5:16 states:

Confess your trespasses to one another, and pray for one another, that you may be healed. The effective, fervent prayer of a righteous man avails much.

Consistent and persistent prayers are vital as you go through your situational sanctuary. Set aside a designated time and place everyday where you can talk and listen to God and not be disturbed. God deserves your undivided attention. When you finish praying and calling on the name of Jesus, be prepared for the enemy to show up in some way, shape, or fashion. Don't worry! God has provided instructions on what you need to do to prepare for the attack:

> *Finally, my brethren, be strong in the Lord and in the power of His might. Put on the whole armor of God, that you may be able to stand against the wiles of the devil. For we do not wrestle against flesh and blood, but against principalities, against powers, against the rulers of the darkness of this age, against spiritual hosts of wickedness in the heavenly places. Therefore take up the whole armor of God, that you may be able to withstand in the evil day, and having done all, to stand.*
>
> *Stand therefore, having girded your waist with truth, having put on the breastplate of righteousness, and having shod your feet with the preparation of the gospel of peace; above all, taking the shield of faith with which you will be able to quench all the fiery darts of the wicked one. And take the helmet of salvation, and the sword of the Spirit, which is the word of God; praying always with all prayer and supplication in the Spirit, being watchful to this end with all perseverance and supplication for all the saints.*

Ephesians 6:10-18

Keep the faith and keep praying until something happens!

3. CRYING IN YOUR SITUATION

When we experience difficult or painful situations in life, crying is a typical response. Whether it is the death of a loved one, unexpected loss of a job or bad doctor's report, crying offers temporary relief to a frustrating or overwhelming situation. Although crying is a natural emotion, many believe that tears in a particular situation represent weakness rather than strength and refrain from displaying this emotion publicly. Many little boys struggle with this because they are taught at an early age not to cry. It makes them appear "weak," "soft" or "girlie". These same little boys grow up to become men that are still afraid to cry.

The bible encourages us to cry out to God. Psalm 34:15 tells us "The eyes of the Lord are on the righteous, and His ears are open to their cry." Psalm 34:17 also says:

The righteous cry out, and the Lord hears, and delivers them out of all their troubles.

When your situation becomes bad enough, no one will have to tell you to cry out to God. It will become a natural instinct.

There was a time in my life when all I could do was cry out to God for help. When my father died in March 2009, I suffered my second miscarriage three weeks later. I could not believe it had happened again! As I lay in my hospital bed one night, my blood pressure elevated to the point of possibly having a stroke. I had been through so much already that I wanted an end to my pain. My heart and body hurt so badly, and I was weak.

During the middle of the morning, something awakened me. As I focused my eyes, I saw my father standing in my room dressed in a black suit looking as healthy as he did before being diagnosed with cancer. He did not say a word. I thought I had seen a ghost. I stared at him because I could not believe my eyes and knew that death was not too far away. I wanted to take his hand and go with him and see my children. My hospital bed was about to become my deathbed.

My nurse called my doctor while I lay there waiting to die. I told Timothy that God was calling me home. As I thought about all the people who depended on and needed me, God gave me strength in my weakness. I slowly swung my legs to the side of the bed and propped myself up on my arms. While I sat there, I prayed for God to lower my blood pressure and spare my life. The nurse injected medication into the IV drip in my arm and returned to take my blood pressure reading. My blood pressure remained elevated, and she would repeat the process. I cried out to God and prayed harder than I have ever prayed because I knew my life depended on it. For two hours (4:30 a.m. until 6:30 a.m.), I prayed Scriptures that I did not know that I knew until my blood pressure decreased to a normal level. Imagine what would have happened if I had lay there and not cried out to God and prayed? This book would not have been written.

My hospital bed became a sanctuary where God revealed his power and glory. During the Fourth Watch, I invited God to do what I could not do. He was my physician, comforter and healer. He restored me and showed me He was in control of the situation. The devil wanted me to believe that my situation was uncontrollable and impossible, but that is not what God said. All I had to do was believe, cry out to God, and pray.

No other person in the bible was better at crying out to God than King David. King David had his faults like many of us but had a heart for God. Many of the Psalms express how he would cry out to God during his times of distress and God answered. He had successes but made some bad choices, which lead to devastating consequences including death of a son. His actions affected not only himself but also his family and the nation. The good news is that God forgave him of his sins. Do you have any sins that are preventing you from crying out to God? God already knows and is waiting for you to confess them and ask for forgiveness.

Sometimes it may seem like the more you cry out to God, the worse the situation becomes. The enemy wants you to believe that God has forgotten you, but that is not true. Deuteronomy 31:6 states:

Be strong and courageous. Do not be afraid or terrified because of them, for the LORD your God goes with you; he will never leave you nor forsake you.

As Moses spoke these words to Joshua, God is speaking them to you. He wants you to stand on his word regardless of your situation. Your situation may look impossible, but you serve an incredible and awesome God that specializes in making the impossible possible. He also never fails.

During your situation, you must continue to cry out to God and stand on his Word. Whether you have been praying for healing of your body, finances, marriage or family and things get worse instead of better, keep the faith. The enemy wants you to become frustrated and angry and give up on God. God knows and understands. He wants you to trust Him. Faith and prayer are the two most powerful tools believers possess. When you don't have these, you are already defeated.

Do not be afraid to cry out to God. He's waiting with open arms and ready to wipe away every tear. When I arrived home after my first miscarriage, I slept downstairs because I was too weak to climb the stairs. At night, Timothy would ask if I wanted him to sleep downstairs with me and I would say no because I wanted to be alone. As I would lay on the couch, I would cry myself to sleep while listening to Bishop Paul Morton's song "Your Tears":

Your tears are just temporary relief.
Your tears are just a release of the pain, sorrow, grief.
Your tears are expressions that can't be controlled.

16

A little crying out is alright,
but after awhile you won't have to cry no more;
don't you worry, God's gonna wipe every tear away.

Chorus 1:
I won't have to cry no more,
I won't have to cry no more,
I won't have to cry no more
when I reach the other shore.

You promised me joy and peace,
oh what a blessed, sweet relief,

Chorus 2:
He's gonna wipe, wipe,
wipe all of my tears away.

Bridge 1:
Weeping may endure for a night,
joy will come in the morning.
Hold on to His unchanging hand,
brand new day is gonna come.

Chorus 2

Bridge 2:
Weeping may endure for a night,
joy will come in the morning.
You've got to hold on
You've got to hold on
You've got to hold on
You've got to hold on
You and you and you and you and you and you and
you and you,
brand new day is gonna come.

Whatever situation you may be facing, it is ok to cry. Depending on your situation, you may go through "The 5 Stages of Loss and Grief." God knows, and He cares. He will wipe away every tear and give you joy. Psalm 30:5 says it best:

Weeping may endure for a night, But joy comes in the morning.

4. TRUSTING GOD WITH YOUR SITUATION

How often have you put your trust in someone or something only to be disappointed? Probably more times than you care to remember. Although trust is a simple five-letter word, it can be difficult sometimes. Trust begins at an early age. When I gave birth to my son, Timothy Jr., the nurse stressed the importance of he and I bonding immediately. She started the process by placing him directly on my chest so that he could remember the familiar sound of my heartbeat that he heard while in the womb. This small step helped him begin to trust and adjust to an unfamiliar environment.

In life, your parents and experiences taught you to not be too trusting of people due to their hidden agendas and motives. You also learned that trust must be earned. Once you began trusting people, you felt comfortable entrusting them with your valuable possessions such as your money, children, health, and even your heart and soul. Being too trusting can sometimes leave you feeling vulnerable as well as violated. Don't think so? Think about all the relationships that tragically end because one person violated the other's trust.

Many organizations spend thousands of dollars on team-building workshops to improve employee bonding and morale. Early in my career, I participated in a team-building workshop that involved the famous trust fall exercise. Employees were assigned partners and took turns falling backwards into their partner's waiting arms. Although there were some successes, I observed some people abruptly hit the floor! The exercise's point encouraged coworkers to work together, trust each other and have each other's back.

Everyone experiences trust issues but why is trust so difficult? Trust requires giving up control of the situation and relying totally on someone or something. Every day you trust that when you get in your car it will start. Sometimes you may have some hesitations depending on whether your car has been malfunctioning but you still hope that it will start.

Isn't it good to know that you can trust God without any hesitations or reservations? Numbers 23:19 states:

God is not a man, that He should lie, Nor a son of man, that He should repent. Has He said, and will He not do? Or has He spoken, and will He not make it good?

Unlike people, God never disappoints even at those times when you may not be able to see it. He is never busy, always available, and always has your best interest in mind.

Trusting God requires that you surrender your will and situation completely to him. It is easy to depend on your intellect and material possessions such as money, cars, job, or social connections, but these things can quickly fade away. Luke 18:18-27 illustrates how the rich young ruler wanted eternal life but could not trust Jesus enough to sell his possessions, give the money to the poor, and follow Him. Many, including you, and myself would probably have difficulty following these instructions. You might become sorrowful like the young ruler, but there are some things that material possessions simply cannot buy. Jesus tested the young ruler to uncover his heart's true treasure along with the strength of his faith. Needless to say, he did not pass the test, and today's generation might not pass either.

When I struggled with infertility and suffered recurrent miscarriages, it became difficult for me to trust God. At that time, I did not understand God's plan for my life or how He would use my adversity to increase my faith and trust in Him. After a miscarriage and before Timothy and I would try again to become pregnant, I prayed to God that I would give birth to a child rather than mourn the loss of another child. I believed, trusted, fasted and prayed but I still suffered three unexplainable recurrent miscarriages. Depression set in, and there were times when I would not leave our home out of fear of crying hysterically upon seeing babies. I was also tormented by images of pregnant women at my OB-GYN office. The devil along with doctors made me believe that my present situation was destined to be my future.

Timothy and I decided to try one last time to have a child. We prayed and found one of the best infertility specialists for our situation. After numerous tests, God revealed that I have hypothyroidism and Polycystic Ovary Syndrome (PCOS), which affected my ability to become pregnant due to hormone imbalance. My doctor prescribed numerous drugs to control it and help me become pregnant. After a year of trying to conceive, nothing happened. My doctor told us that we would have to "pullout the big guns" and try some infertility treatments such as Intrauterine Insemination (IUI) or In Vitro Fertilization (IVF). These treatments cost between $10,000 and $15,000 per cycle and only have a 30%-40% success rate. We were not willing to make that investment for such a small return on investment. Also, my spirit was uneasy about pursuing this path. Our hopes and dreams for having a child died in his office that August day.

My doctor wanted to run some additional blood work tests just in case we changed our minds. Our nurse entered the room, and I could not believe my eyes. She was pregnant! How did I miss it? All I could think was how could God be so cruel. After she had drawn my blood, I immediately hurried to the bathroom down the hall. I closed the stall door behind me and cried. I was frustrated and disgusted from four years of trying to become pregnant. When was my time going to come? I composed myself, and we drove home in silence. When we reached a particular interstate exit, I uncontrollably burst into tears again. I could not believe that this was happening.

Once I arrived home, I began tossing out all the remaining ovulation kits. I decided it was time to quit. I gave it my best, but it was not meant to be. As I was angrily tossing the ovulation kits in the trashcan, God spoke this thought to me:

It is not your job to set a timetable for me to move. Your job is to only trust, believe, and obey.

I immediately froze because I could not believe what I heard. I looked around and called out for Timothy, but I was the only one home. From that moment, I learned that God's timing is not my timing. He may not always move at the time I ask or when I need him to, but he is faithful. As the lyrics of Dottie Peoples' song, "On Time God" say:

He may not come when you want Him,
but he'll be there right on time.
He's an on time God, yes he is!

Three months later, I was pregnant and back in my doctor's office. When he came in to see me, he said, "This is one special baby! I never said I knew more than God!"

Whatever you are facing right now, trust God with it. Begin to meditate on Proverbs 3:5-6:

Trust in the Lord with all your heart, and lean not on your own understanding; In all your ways acknowledge Him, And He shall direct your paths.

Your present situation may seem like it will never end or improve, but it will. It is only temporary:

For our light affliction, which is but for a moment, is working for us a far more exceeding and eternal weight of glory, while we do not look at the things which are seen, but at the things which are not seen. For things which are seen are temporary, but the things which are not seen are eternal .

2 Corinthians 4:17

The enemy wants you to think that God has forgotten and abandoned you. God sees and knows all that you are facing, but he is waiting for you to call, surrender and trust Him. By the world's standards, you must see something before you believe but that is not how God works. With God, you must first believe before you see something happen. 2 Corinthians 5:7 states:

For we walk by faith, not by sight.

When I discovered I was pregnant, I walked by faith

and not by sight. Based on my history, fear and anxiety weighed heavily on me. The farthest I had gone in my previous pregnancies was 20 weeks and I started wondering how far would I make it this time. I immediately started praying that God would keep my unborn child and myself safe and let him or her be born healthy. I began meditating on 2 Timothy 1:7:

> *For God has not given us a spirit of fear, but of power and of love and of a sound mind.*

At every doctor's visit during the ultrasound, I would look up at the ceiling and quote faith Scriptures in my mind. Everything seemed to be going well until 18 weeks. During a routine ultrasound, we found out that our son had a hole at the top of his heart that would either close on its own or require surgery. How could this be happening? I felt as if God ignored my prayers.

I walked by faith and trusted God to close the hole. In the meantime, I began anointing my stomach and praying over our son numerous times throughout the day. On July 19, 2012, God delivered Timothy Jr. (TJ) at 38 weeks when doctors told me if I did get pregnant again, I might only make it to 27 weeks. My husband and I rejoiced over the miraculous blessing that God had blessed us with, but the enemy had other plans. One of the hospital's on call cardiologist informed us that the hole was still there. Our journey was only beginning.

Every other week, we took TJ to the cardiologist for heart ultrasounds along with visits to his pediatrician. I dispensed medicines at different intervals throughout the day and had to use a medicine reminder app on my iPhone to stay on schedule. As young as TJ was, he started refusing the medicines by pressing his lips tightly together. These were some long days and sleepless nights.

In November 2012, TJ's cardiologist called and told me that TJ needed to have open-heart surgery. Although I knew this day was coming, I still was not prepared for it. We scheduled it for early December because we wanted him home for Thanksgiving and Christmas. The closer the surgery date approached, the more nervous I became. I prayed for God to bless me with a healthy child, but I was not prepared for this. Or so I thought. We prayed and so did our Pastor and church family for God to guide the surgeon's hands during the operation. It was a terribly stressful time.

On December 6, 2012 at 5:30 a.m., the Children's Healthcare of Atlanta Chapel became our sanctuary. We needed God like never before. With tears streaming down our faces, we prayed for God to be in the midst of the operation and keep TJ safe. When the time had come, we kissed four-month-old TJ goodbye and handed him to a nurse to take to the operating room. After four and a half hours, the operation was successful, and TJ was moved to Intensive Care.

During my darkest moments at Children's Healthcare, God sent angels to comfort and encourage me. While I sat at TJ's bedside in Intensive Care, one of the nurses would come over, rest her hand on my shoulder, and ask if I needed anything. She reassured me that everything was going to be fine. As TJ's surgeon walked through the Intensive Care Unit, he would ask if he could get me anything. At those times when I thought I could not go on, God gave me strength to endure. Isaiah 41:10 confirms this:

> *Fear not, for I am with you; Be not dismayed, for I am your God. I will strengthen you, Yes, I will help you, I will uphold you with My righteous right hand.*

No matter what you may be going through and how bad the situation may look, trust God. Psalm 37:3-4 says:

Trust in the Lord, and do good; Dwell in the land, and feed on His faithfulness. Delight yourself also in the Lord, And He shall give you the desires of your heart.

At those times when you feel like you want to quit and give up, read Psalm 91: 1-6:

He who dwells in the secret place of the Most High
Shall abide under the shadow of the Almighty.
I will say of the LORD, "He is my refuge and my fortress;
My God, in Him I will trust."
Surely He shall deliver you from the snare of the fowler
And from the perilous pestilence.
He shall cover you with His feathers,
And under His wings you shall take refuge;
His truth shall be your shield and buckler.
You shall not be afraid of the terror by night,
Nor of the arrow that flies by day,
Nor of the pestilence that walks in darkness,
Nor of the destruction that lays waste at noonday.

My brothers and sisters, you are not alone. God is with you and will carry you through! I'm reminded of the hymn "Yield Not To Temptation" by Horatio Palmer that will help you fight the good fight of faith during your situation:

Yield not to temptation, for yielding is sin;
Each vict'ry will help you some other to win;
Fight manfully onward, dark passions subdue;
Look ever to Jesus, He'll carry you through.

Refrain:
Ask the Savior to help you,
Comfort, strengthen, and keep you;
He is willing to aid you,
He will carry you through.

Shun evil companions, bad language disdain,
God's name hold in rev'rence, nor take it in vain;
Be thoughtful and earnest, kindhearted and true;
Look ever to Jesus, He'll carry you through.

To him that o'ercometh, God giveth a crown,
Through faith we will conquer, though often cast
down;
He who is our Savior, our strength will renew;
Look ever to Jesus, He'll carry you through.

5. RELEASING YOUR SITUATION

Do you have a tendency to hold onto things rather than releasing them? I do. Everyone struggles with this whether they admit it or not. If you are like me, you try to solve your problems but sometimes end up making things worse instead of better. I learned the hard way that when you have tried everything but to no avail, you must release it. God cannot come into your situation and move as long as you hold onto it. Psalms 55:22 says:

Cast your burden on the LORD, And He shall sustain you; He shall never permit the righteous to be moved.

God does not need your help with your situation but requires your participation. He needs you to do those things that He equipped you to do and rely on him for those things that only he can do. In today's vernacular, God needs you to "stay in your lane." For example, you may be unemployed and been praying and looking for a job for quite some time with no success. Have you released it to God? Once you release your situation completely to God, you must still do your part. You must continue to operate in faith, pray and believe that God will bless you with a job, but do not stop looking. Continue looking and networking for a job. Even when it seems as if nothing is working, you keep telling yourself "Today is going to be the day." Hold fast to Matthew 17:20:

So Jesus said to them, "Because of your unbelief; for assuredly, I say to you, if you have faith as a mustard seed, you will say to this mountain, 'Move from here to there,' and it will move; and nothing will be impossible for you.

One of my favorite Scriptures involves Elisha the Prophet and the widow in 2 Kings 4:1-7. The widow's husband, a prophet, passed away, and creditors were coming to take her two sons as slaves because she did not have the money to pay her debts. Can you imagine how many people today would lose their children due to not having the money to pay their debts? Too many to count! On the other hand, some would gladly yell "take my children!"

The widow knew she could not solve this problem so God leads her to the right person who could help with her situation. After she had explained her situation to Elisha, he gave her specific instructions:

Then he said "Go, borrow vessels from everywhere, from all your neighbors – empty vessels; do not gather just a few. And when you have come in, you shall shut the door behind you and your sons; then pour it into all those vessels, and set aside the full ones."

2 Kings 4:3

She could have told him that this sounded crazy and did not make sense, but her situation was so critical, she believed, trusted and released it by seeking out one of God's messengers. Although Elisha could have solved her situation himself, he provided her with instructions to solve her problem. She did not just release her situation to God, sit back and do nothing. She and her sons actively participated in their blessing and obediently followed Elisha's instructions:

So she went from him and shut the door behind her and her sons, who brought the vessels to her; and she poured it out. Now it came to pass, when the vessels were full, that she said to her son, "Bring me another vessel." And he said to her, "There is not another vessel." So the oil ceased.

2 Kings 4:5-6

Her situation transformed itself into a sanctuary where God appeared and multiplied the small amount of oil she had until there were no more vessels. She and her sons experienced the miracle firsthand and knew that no one but God could have done this. It is one thing for someone to tell you about God's miraculous power, but it is something different to experience it yourself.

After I had exhausted all of my resources and power to have a child, and nothing worked, I released it into God's hands. I told God that if He blessed me with a child I would be fine but even if he did not, I would have to learn to accept and deal with it. At this point, I was tired of doing the same thing expecting a different result which is the definition of insanity. After releasing it to God, I decided that I would try a different approach. I searched the Scriptures and found one that spoke directly to my situation, Psalm 127:3:

Behold, children are a heritage from the LORD, The fruit of the womb is a reward.

I began to meditate on it day and night and included it in my daily prayer time to remind God of his promise. Since there are strength and power in numbers, I decided to solicit the help of my church's prayer warriors to intercede on my behalf. I wrote my anonymous prayer request and placed it in the prayer basket during the offertory period. After that, I did not think about having a child anymore. Instead, I continued to serve within my church and meditate on my Scripture. I also decided that I would be the best role model I could be to the children that I interacted with in my Sunday School class. When you busy yourself doing the things of God, you do not have time to worry or stress about things that may or may not be going right in your life but start enjoying and living life. Philippians 4:8 says it this way:

Finally, brethren, whatever things are true, whatever things are noble, whatever things are just, whatever things are pure, whatever things are lovely, whatever things are of good report, if there is any virtue and if there is anything praiseworthy—meditate on these things.

The Sunday evening after Thanksgiving, I watched Pastor Joel Osteen of Lakewood Church on television. In one segment of his message, he addressed how some people complain about their children getting on their nerves while others wish they had children to get on their nerves. He went on to say how many people have tried everything to have children with no success. I emphatically agreed with him by saying "Amen!" After he made that statement, something in my spirit spoke to me and said "That is not you anymore." It startled me and made me think. What if I am pregnant? Immediately, I rose from the couch and went upstairs to our bathroom to locate one remaining pregnancy test. I found one and took the test. While sitting on the side of our tub waiting for the result, I started planning my week. When it was time to check the results, I stood up and looked at the test: positive. I could not believe my eyes!

I ran downstairs to tell Timothy the news. He was stunned. I called my doctor's office the next day, and they faxed lab orders to a LabCorp office near our home. Once the lab results confirmed my pregnancy, my reproductive endocrinologist's office scheduled me an appointment. Timothy and I knew that we had a long journey ahead, but we had to walk by faith and not by sight and apply Philippians 3:13-14:

> *Brethren, I do not count myself to have apprehended; but one thing I do, forgetting those things which are behind and reaching forward to those things which are ahead, I press toward the goal for the prize of the upward call of God in Christ Jesus.*

At the appointment, everything was looking good but Timothy and I were anxious and nervous. We had been at this point too many times before only to be disappointed. At this point, God was the only one who could make this pregnancy last the full duration. It was too late to turn back now.

Once my appointment ended, I proceeded to the checkout desk. I will never forget the woman who helped me that day. She noticed on my paperwork that I was pregnant and said "Congratulations! What did you use to get pregnant? IVF or IUI?" I said "Neither. I used GOD." Her response was "That doesn't seem fair!" I responded "Unfortunately; you do not know my story."

Similar to the woman I encountered, many will never know your story to understand God's glory in your life. The power of release is not always easy but is necessary for God to step into your situation and move. Don't delay your breakthrough and blessings any longer by holding onto it. Once you release it to God, understand that the outcome may or may not be favorable or what you expect. When I released my father's illness to God, I fasted and prayed and trusted and believed God to heal his body. In March 2009, my father passed away two days before his 64th birthday. I realized years later that God did answer my prayer and healed him but not in the earthly realm which I had hoped. My father is no longer suffering and will never have to experience pain and sickness again. God changed my perspective concerning the situation, which gave me peace. He can do the same for you. Why not release your situation to him today? You do not have anything to lose, but everything to gain.

6. PRAISING AND WORSHIPPING

No matter how much faith you possess, life's situations can overwhelm you, hijack your thoughts and replay numerous times in your mind like a sitcom rerun. By the time it is all said and done, you have no room to think about anything else. You may question God and your faith. You may press your way to God's sanctuary to praise and worship Him, fellowship with other believers and hear a word from God, but your situation consumes you to the point that it is all you think about. You cannot enjoy the service or the sermon. At times, you may feel as if you have a dark cloud above your head following you but do not forget above your head is the source of your help. Psalm 121:1-4 says:

> *I will lift up my eyes to the hills from whence comes my help? My help comes from the LORD, Who made heaven and earth. He will not allow your foot to be moved; He who keeps you will not slumber.*

While you are going through your situation, the devil tries to make every day seem dark, dreary, and dismal to keep you in bondage and steal your joy and hope but do not forget that God can work miracles in dark places and spaces. Remember Paul and Silas? They were stripped of their clothes and beaten for casting out a demonic spirit from a slave girl that allowed her to predict the future. She no longer possessed this money-making ability for her masters, which enraged them. They held Paul and Silas responsible for terminating their income source and initiated the process of having them thrown in jail. Placed in jail and feet placed in stocks, Paul and Silas were in a bad and dark situation, but this did not stop their praise:

But at midnight Paul and Silas were praying and singing hymns to God, and the prisoners were listening to them. Suddenly there was a great earthquake, so that the foundations of the prison were shaken; and immediately all the doors were opened and everyone's chains were loosed.

Acts 16:25-26

If Paul's and Silas' praise caused an earthquake, imagine what your praise and worship could do? If they could praise God while in jail, you should be able to give Him praise despite your situation. You might be facing cancer, divorce, foreclosure, debt, unruly children, or job loss but God deserves the praise. I call this type of praise "in spite of praise." In spite of having cancer, praise God. In spite of your marriage crumbling, praise God. In spite of not having enough money to pay your bills or buy food, praise God. In spite of your body filled with pain, praise God. In spite of how you feel, praise God. In spite of not knowing what to do, praise God.

The disciples encountered rough winds and waves on the Sea of Galilee while in their boat. Jesus appeared before them walking on the water:

Now in the fourth watch of the night Jesus went to them, walking on the sea. And when the disciples saw Him walking on the sea, they were troubled, saying, "It is a ghost!" And they cried out for fear. But immediately Jesus spoke to them, saying, "Be of good cheer! It is I; do not be afraid."

Matthew 14:25-27

The fourth watch represents one of four Roman three-hour interval watches from 3:00 a.m. until 6:00 a.m. called morning. When the disciples set out in their boat on the sea, everything was good. It was only when they got to the middle that they encountered trouble. Your situation may be similar. Your finances may have been good at the beginning of the year but towards the middle of the year you lost your job. Perhaps, you may have been in good health and enjoying life at the beginning of the year when your doctor unexpectedly diagnosed you with cancer or some other devastating health condition. Like the disciples soon discovered and so will you, Jesus can appear in the most hopeless and desperate situations.

No matter how bad your situation may seem, something good can come out of it. Even though I experienced three miscarriages before having my son, God strengthened my faith and revealed my underlying thyroid and PCOS conditions. Peter experienced something good that he might not otherwise have experienced if it was not for the storm:

And Peter answered Him and said, "Lord, if it is You, command me to come to You on the water." So He said, "Come." And when Peter had come down out of the boat, he walked on the water to go to Jesus. But when he saw that the wind was boisterous, he was afraid; and beginning to sink he cried out saying, "Lord, save me!" An immediately Jesus stretched out His hand and caught him, and said to him, "O you of little faith, why did you doubt?" And when they got into the boat, the wind ceased .

Matthew 14:28-32

Jesus revealed his power to Peter by allowing Peter to walk on water, but Peter had to do three things: ask, believe, and step out. It took faith on Peter's part to want to walk on water. He could have been like the other disciples and been content with staying in the boat and waiting for their demise or the storm to cease. Staying in the boat represented a comfortable and familiar surrounding compared to the unknown conditions outside of the boat. You could choose to remain in your situation without ever encountering the presence and power of God but why would you want that? Keep your focus on God, and he will sustain you no matter what you may be going through. Peter only began sinking when he took his eyes off of Jesus and focused on his surroundings. Once you take your eyes off of God during your situation, you could potentially sink into depression, despair, drug abuse, bitterness or more.

> *Then those who were in the boat came and worshipped Him, saying "Truly You are the Son of God."*
>
> Matthew 14:33

It is good to praise and worship God after being delivered from your storm but oftentimes you must praise and worship your way through the storm. Gospel recording artist and minister, Marvin Sapp, sings a song titled "Praise Him In Advance." In the song's introduction, he warns against waiting until your situation is over to praise God. He refers to these types of praisers as "conditional praisers." He encourages believers that despite their situation to praise God in advance. What type of praiser are you?

I was a conditional praiser until I matured in my Christian walk and encountered many faith-building storms. I understand now that no matter how my situation looks or the obstacles placed before me, I must believe and trust God to deliver and bless me but I must praise and worship Him. Remember the familiar saying "When praises go up, blessings come down?" or "God inhabits the praises of his people?" Psalm 150:1-6 says:

Praise the LORD!
Praise God in His sanctuary;
Praise Him in His mighty firmament!
Praise Him for His mighty acts;
Praise Him according to His excellent greatness!
Praise Him with the sound of the trumpet;
Praise Him with the lute and harp!
Praise Him with the timbrel and dance;
Praise Him with stringed instruments and flutes!
Praise Him with loud cymbals;
Praise Him with clashing cymbals!
Let everything that has breath praise the LORD.
Praise the LORD!

What does it mean to praise God? John 4:24 reveals "God is Spirit, and those who worship Him must worship in spirit and truth." Praise begins on the inside and manifests itself on the outside. Many believers wait until they enter the sanctuary to praise God and worship Him, but God desires your praises wherever you may be. Whether you are driving in your car or shopping in the grocery store, give God some praise for the great things he has done. If you do not praise God, the rocks will cry out in your place (Luke 19:40). Praise God at all times!

How do you praise God? Hallelujah is the highest praise that you can give God. Become an instrument or vessel of praise. God desires authentic praise. Hebrews 13:15 says:

Therefore by Him let us continually offer the sacrifice of praise to God, that is, the fruit of our lips, giving thanks to His name.

But do not forget to do good and to share, for with such sacrifices God is well pleased.

You also praise God by lifting, waving and clapping your hands. Psalm 47:1-2 states:

Oh, clap your hands, all you peoples! Shout to God with the voice of triumph! For the LORD Most High is awesome; He is a great King over all the earth.

In Psalm 28:2, David says:

Hear the voice of my supplications When I cry to You, When I lift up my hands toward Your holy sanctuary.

David also speaks of praising God through dancing and singing in Psalm 30:11-12:

You have turned for me my mourning into dancing; You have put off my sackcloth and clothed me with gladness, To the end that my glory may sing praise to You and not be silent. O LORD my God, I will give thanks to You forever.

Always express thanksgiving and gratitude to God with your mouth and in your prayers. Never take for granted the goodness, grace, and mercy of God because it is a privilege that many do not receive. While I was going through my situational sanctuary with miscarriages, I learned to praise God for just being God. I began to praise him for all the wonderful things he had done in my life along with the things that he would do. When I suffered my last miscarriage in September 2013, God gave me strength that allowed me to handle it much better than previous ones. When depression tried to overtake me, God used TJ to lift my spirits with a smile and a hug. Whatever your situational sanctuary is today, give God praise for bringing it to you and know that He can bring you through it. There is power in the name of Jesus! He knows how much you can bear. Don't let the enemy steal your praise!

7. TESTIFYING

You probably have attended church services where members stood in front of the congregation and gave their testimony. During or after the testimony, you might have overheard people saying things like, "I never would have shared that" or "She shared too much information." Once you stop trying to satisfy so-called saints and focus on saving souls, God will use you and your testimony in ways you cannot imagine. When you realize that you will not please everyone no matter what you do or how hard you try, you free yourself to be used by God.

When God delivers you from a situation, you may have a tendency to keep your testimony to yourself. Depending on the situation God delivered you from and how He delivered you, you might feel ashamed or unworthy and not want anyone to know out of fear of being judged or looked at differently. To fully be used by God for the building of his kingdom, you must put your ego and pride aside and put the needs of healing, delivering, and setting others free first.

For several years, I would not talk about my

miscarriages because I blamed myself and felt less than a woman. The bible instructs us "to be fruitful and multiply" but I could not. Anytime someone asked me, "Do you have any children?" or "Why don't you have any children?", I wrestled with the response because unless people have walked in your shoes, they will not truly understand. In other words, they can sympathize but not empathize. As a result, I put my mask on every Sunday and any other time I would encounter this question. I learned how to smile on the outside while being tormented on the inside.

The enemy wanted me to have a pity party instead of a praise party so that he could destroy my faith and trust in God. You owe it to your fellow believers to encourage them through your testimony about God's goodness, grace, mercy, and favor. Stop worrying about what people will think or say. God's opinion is the only one that matters. Be obedient to God's word and proclaim his love to others. John 3:16 tells of God's love for humanity along with his greatest sacrifice:

> *For God so loved the world that He gave His only begotten Son that whoever believes in Him should not perish but have everlasting life.*

Revelations 12:11 speaks of this sacrifice in regards to overcoming the enemy:

> *And they overcame him by the blood of the Lamb and by the word of their testimony, and they did not love their lives to death.*

Each test or trial in your life is an opportunity for a testimony. One of my favorite songs is Andrae Crouch's "Through It All." Although it can be difficult when you are being tested, verse three addresses how believers should look at various storms and tests in their lives:

I thank God for the mountains,
and I thank him for the valleys,
I thank Him for the storms He brought me through.
For if I'd never had a problem,
I wouldn't know God could solve them,
I'd never know what faith in God could do.

When God steps into your situation and delivers you, you cannot help but to tell someone. When Jesus healed a leper in Mark 1:40-45, he gave the leper specific instructions:

> *And He strictly warned him and sent him away at once, and said to him, "See that you say nothing to anyone; but go your way, show yourself to the priest, and offer for your cleansing those things which Moses commanded, as a testimony to them. However, he went out and began to proclaim it freely, and to spread the matter, so that Jesus could no longer openly enter the city, but was outside in deserted places; and they came to Him from every direction.*

I understand the leper's enthusiasm for spreading the news about his healing. He wanted others to know that the man named Jesus healed him and could do the same for them. Shouldn't this be the basis for our testimony to encourage other believers that might be going through a similar situation? Why not "rejoice with those that rejoice and mourn with those who mourn" (Romans 12:15)?

When was the last time you shared a testimony with someone? God's glory is in your story and others need to hear it. Maybe God healed you from Stage 4 cancer when doctors gave up on you? Maybe God blessed your finances after you lost your job? Maybe He allowed you to walk away from a car accident that should have killed you? Become a living testimony for God! Another one of my favorite songs is by Rev. Clay Evans titled "I've Got A

Testimony":

SOLOIST:
As I look back over my life
And I think things over I can truly say that I've been
blessed
I've got a testimony
(REPEAT)

CHOIR:
As I look back over my life
And I think things over I can truly say that I've been
blessed
I've got a testimony
(REPEAT)

SOLOIST:
Sometimes I couldn't see my way through
But the Lord He brought me out
Right now I'm free
I've got the victory
I've got a testimony
(REPEAT)

CHOIR:
As I look back over my life
And I think things over I can truly say that I've been
blessed
I've got a testimony
(REPEAT)

Make today the day that you bless someone with your
testimony. Someone needs to hear it.

CONCLUSION

In life, everyone experiences situations. Some of these will be good while others will be bad. Many books have been written on the subject of suffering and why a loving God allows it in believers' lives. God wants to make sure that we are not giving him lip service but are willing to suffer as disciples of Jesus Christ.

Instead of focusing on the bad in a bad situation, look at the situation from God's perspective. From His perspective, it is a situational sanctuary where He can reveal himself to you through His Son, Jesus Christ.

No one likes adversity, but no one is exempt. When adversity comes in your life through various situations, remember Proverbs 24:10:

If you faint in the day of adversity, Your strength is small.

Call on your Lord and Savior, Jesus Christ for strength to endure:

Blessed be the LORD,
Because He has heard the voice of my supplications!
The LORD is my strength and my shield;
My heart trusted in Him, and I am helped;
Therefore my heart greatly rejoices,
And with my song I will praise Him.

Psalm 28:6-7

I hope that the information shared in these pages blessed you and renewed your strength and faith as you go through your situational sanctuary. There will be valley experiences, but you cannot stay there. Strive to make it to the mountaintop where you can raise your arms and say "Hallelujah! Look where God brought me from and look where he brought me to!"

I would love to hear from you! Please share your thoughts and testimonies by emailing me at authorlisasims@icloud.com. Also, don't forget to leave a review on Amazon, follow me on Twitter (@bizmoneysaver and @authorlisasims) and visit my websites, authorlisasims.com or stretchingyourcash.com.

God bless you and keep you until we meet again!

PRAYER RESOURCES

Prayer is one of the most powerful tools in a Christian's arsenal. Without it, you cannot defeat the enemy and declare victory in your situation. Prayer changes things! Here are a few resources that I use to strengthen my prayer life that can do the same for you:

Books

- Simple Prayer – Joyce Meyer

- Authority in Prayer – Dutch Sheets

- Power Prayers to Start Your Day – Donna K. Maltese

- What Happens When Women Pray – Evelyn Christenson

- Prayer The Great Adventure – David Jeremiah

- A Journey Into Prayer - Evelyn Christenson

- Prayer – Your Foundation For Success – Kenneth Copeland

- Your Prayers – A Guidebook to a More Powerful Prayer Life - Andrew Murray, Toni Sortor and Pamela L. McQuade

- A 12-Month Guide To Better Prayer

LISA'S IPHONE PLAYLIST

When I'm going through situational sanctuaries, I listen to music to comfort and minister to my soul. I transform my car into a sanctuary where music fills the air. There is always a song that can be applied to your situation that will soothe, comfort, and speak to you and remind you of God's power. Here's a listing of some of my favorite songs that I keep in rotation on a daily basis:

Determination
- Souled Out - Hezekiah Walker & LFC

Faithfulness
- Great Is Thy Faithfulness – Earnest Pugh
- Faithful Is Our God – Hezekiah Walker

Guidance
- Don't Do It Without Me – Bishop Paul Morton
- Lead Me, Guide Me – Jeff Majors

Praise And Worship
- Every Praise – Hezekiah Walker

- Church Medley – Bishop Gregory Davis
- Victory Is Mine – Dorothy Norwood
- My Name Is Victory – Jonathan Nelson
- Can't Nobody Do Me Like Jesus – Rev. James Cleveland
- Amazing – Ricky Dillard
- High Praise – Essence of Praise and Worship
- Hallelujah Anyhow – Rev. Clay Evans
- He Has Done Great Things - James Abbington
- Hallelujah You're Worthy – Judith Christie McAllister
- Praise Him In Advance – Marvin Sapp
- Great Jesus – Kurt Carr
- I Love To Praise Him – Marvin Sapp
- I Never Lost My Praise – Tramaine Hawkins
- I Will Bless The Lord – Byron Cage
- I've Got A Testimony – Rev. Clay Evans
- Incredible God/Praise – Youthful Praise
- It Will Never Lose Its Power – Rev. Gerald Thompson
- Jesus, I'll Never Forget – Carlton Pearson
- Just Want To Praise You – Maurette Brown Clark
- Like The Dew – Judith Christie McAllister
- God Is Good – Chester D.T. Baldwin
- And We Are Glad – Joe Pace
- Awesome – Pastor Charles Jenkins
- Hymns Medley – Bishop Leonard Scott
- Bless That Wonderful Name – Rev. Ronnie Strong
- Come Thou Almighty King – Minister Keith Armstead
- Celebration Medley – Saints In Praise
- Lord I Thank You – Joyful Praise
- Give Him Glory – Deandre Patterson

Protection
- Safety – Gospel Music Workshop of America

Release
- Let Go – DeWayne Woods
- All In His Hands – Rev. Charles G. Hayes

Strength
- Rock and Shield – Gerald Thompson
- Rough Side of the Mountain – Rev. F.C. Barnes & Rev. Janice Brown
- Something On The Inside – Bishop G.E. Patterson
- Lord, Help Me To Hold Out – Rev. James Cleveland
- Leaning On The Everlasting Arm – Rev. Timothy Wright

Trust
- I Can Depend On God – Rev. Charles H. Nicks, Jr.
- I Can Go To God In Prayer – Albertina Walker
- I Got A Feeling – Albertina Walker
- I Know The Lord Will – Bishop G.E. Patterson
- I Trust You – James Fortune and FIYA
- I Will Trust In The Lord – Rev. James Moore
- Jesus Can Work It Out – Dr. Charles G. Hayes
- Said He Would Be With Me – Elements of Praise & Isaiah D. Thomas
- Pray For Me – The Mighty Clouds of Joy
- All Things Work Together – Malcolm Williams & Great Faith
- The Lord Is Blessing Me – Bishop Larry Trotter

ABOUT THE AUTHOR

Lisa Sims is the host of *The Stretching A Dollar For Entrepreneurs Show* on Blogtalkradio.com where she provides money-saving tips for entrepreneurs on a variety of topics. She is also the creator and host of The Saving Station Podcast (available in iTunes) where she saves consumers money and time and provides a little wisdom for the soul. Likewise, Lisa is an Online Computer Science Instructor for Grantham University and Online Adjunct Instructor for The University of Phoenix Online and Excelsior College where she teaches computer science, web design and project management courses. Likewise, she is a freelance Business and Technology Writer for **Demand Media Studios.** For more information, visit www.stretchingyourcash.com.

OTHER BOOKS BY LISA SIMS

- *Digital Coupon Savings 411*

- *How To Draw People To Your Website (September 2014)*

- *Stretching A Dollar To Save And Make Thousands: An Entrepreneur's Guide To Doing More With Less*

- *Start The Way You Want To Finish: Strategies For Eliminating Excuses And Taking Control*

- *50 Ways To Relax For Busy Moms*

Download QR code reader such as Scanlife to view!